Just to say thanks for downloading my book, I would like to give you the audio book version 100% free.

https://chelseak532002550.wordpress.com

Copyright 2021 Chelsea Kong

All rights reserved. All images used in this book are licensed copies from their respectful owners including myself and includes artwork from Freepik. This book or any portion thereof may not be reproduced or used in any manner whatsoever without the express written permission of the publisher except for the use of brief quotations in a book review.

Printed in 2021, Made in Toronto, Canada
ISBN:978-1-990399-03-9
Legal Deposit, Library and Archives Canada

Table of Contents

Lesson 1: How God Speaks	4-13
Lesson 2: Still Small Voice	14-21
Lesson 3: Audible Voice	22-29
Lesson 4: Feelings	30-37
Lesson 5: Visions	38-45
Lesson 6: Dreams	46-53
Lesson 7: God's Word/Bible	54-59
Lesson 8: God's Thoughts	60-67
Lesson 9: Gift of Prophecy	68-75
Lesson 10: Others	76-83
Lesson 11: Jesus	84-89
Lesson 12: Holy Spirit and His gifts	90-94
Prayer	95
Salvation Prayer	96
Holy Spirit Baptism Prayer	97
Message from the Author	98
Biography	99
Other Products	100
Coaching Products	101

Lesson 1: How God Speaks

Why do we need to hear God?

He wants us to know Him.

He wants to tell us things.

To share with others about Him.

We will be safe from danger.

What you need to hear Him?

You need to read the Bible every day.

Pray every day.

Go to church every week.

Know who God is.

Make time to hear Him.

Books you will need

How to Hear God's Voice for school aged children.

Hear God Speak Young children.

You need to read it on your own time.

Before you begin, pray to the Lord to open your ears, eyes, mind, feelings, and heart to hear Him.

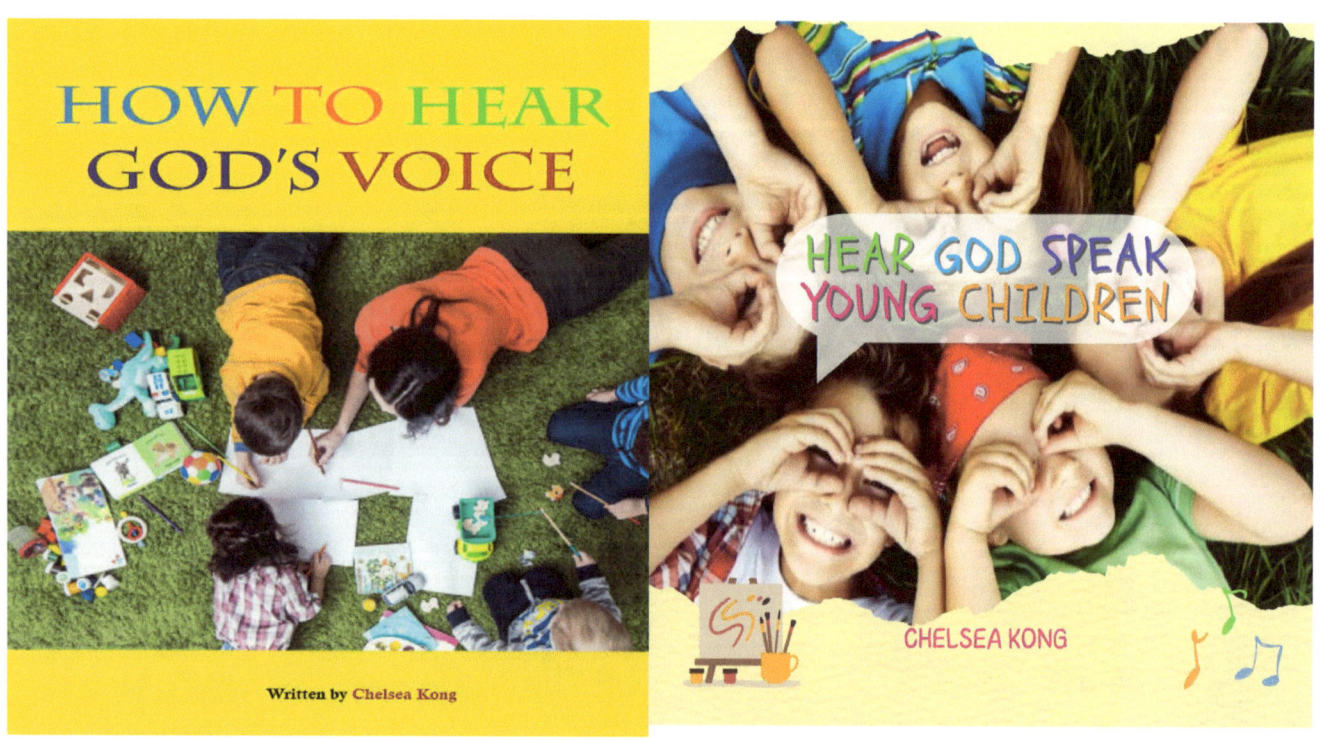

Steps you need to take

Make sure you Know God's Word; the Bible well.

It is better to hear Him in a quiet place alone.

Always be ready to hear Him when He speaks.

Keys to Hear God

Be quiet and make sure your mind is clear.

Believe that He will speak.

Relax and wait for Him to Speak to you.

Picture Jesus talking to you.

He shows us things He wants us to know.

Steps you need to take

Make sure you Know God's Word; the Bible well.

It is better to hear Him in a quiet place alone.

Always be ready to hear Him when He speaks.

Keys to Hear God

Be quiet and make sure your mind is clear.

Believe that He will speak.

Relax and wait for Him to Speak to you.

Picture Jesus talking to you.

He shows us things He wants us to know.

The ways He Speaks

Still small voice

Audible voice

Feelings

Visions

Dreams

Other ways He Speaks

Thoughts

Gift of Prophecy

Others

Jesus

Holy Spirit and His gifts

Practical Exercise

We will take this time to practice.

You can sit, stand, or lie down.

Imagine yourself now with Jesus that He is talking to you.

What you should do

If you have not read either book, you need to take time to do that.

It will tell you more about How to Hear God's Voice.

This lesson is a summary and guide to help you use the steps from the book.

Lesson 2: Still Small Voice

Holy Spirit speaks

Holy Spirit is also gentle like a dove.

He will tell us about Jesus.

He will tell us in love.

You need Him to Hear God better.

Still Small Voice

God speaks to our spirit.

He can use a gentle quiet voice.

We will know it is Him.

He speaks with love.

Still Small Voice

We must be quiet to hear it.

We need to be let God speak when He wants to.

It can be easy to miss what He says.

He will not force us to do what He says.

Still Small Voice

God speaks to our spirit.

He can use a gentle quiet voice.

We will know it is Him.

He speaks with love.

Still Small Voice

We must be quiet to hear it.

We need to be let God speak when He wants to.

It can be easy to miss what He says.

He will not force us to do what He says.

Still Small Voice

Then the Lord said to Elijah, "Go. Stand in front of me on the mountain. I will pass by you." Then a very strong wind blew. It caused the mountains to break apart. It broke apart large rocks in front of the Lord. But the Lord was not in the wind. After the wind, there was an earthquake. But the Lord was not in the earthquake. After the earthquake, there was a fire. But the Lord was not in the fire. After the fire, there was a quiet, gentle voice. When Elijah heard it, he covered his face with his coat. He went out and stood at the entrance to the cave. (1 Kings 19:11-12)

What God may say: Still Small Voice

I love you.

I want you to spend more time with me.

I want you to pray and read the Bible.

Wait a little longer.

Trust me.

How to Know His Still Small Voice

He will always give you peace, joy, and love.

He will repeat what He says to help you.

He is patient and knows your heart.

Practical Exercise

Let's try to hear God's still small voice.

Be ready to stay quiet to listen.

Then write, draw, or record what God shows you.

Lesson 3: Audible Voice

Audible Voice of God

He sounds like Daddy talking.

You can hear from inside you.

You can feel His voice when He speaks.

You hear Him, but don't see Him.

Audible Voice of God

You may get scared.

Your body knows.

It gets you to stop and listen.

Audible Voice of God

The Lord's voice is heard over the sea. The glorious God thunders.   The Lord thunders over the great ocean. The Lord's voice is powerful. The Lord's voice is majestic. The Lord's voice breaks the trees. The Lord breaks the cedars of Lebanon.6 He makes the land of Lebanon dance like a calf. He makes Mount Hermon jump like a baby bull. The Lord's voice makes the lightning flash. The Lord's voice shakes the desert. The Lord shakes the Desert of Kadesh. The Lord's voice shakes the oaks. The leaves fall off the trees. In his Temple everyone says, "Glory to God!" (Psalm 29:3-9)

Audible Voice of God

God's voice has power.

Our spirit man knows when He speaks.

He will warn us of danger.

He directs our steps daily and clearly.

Audible Voice of God

Moses and God's chosen leaders and prophets heard His audible voice.

God gave the 10 Commandments to Moses this way.

God warned His people.

The children of Israel were afraid to hear God speak.

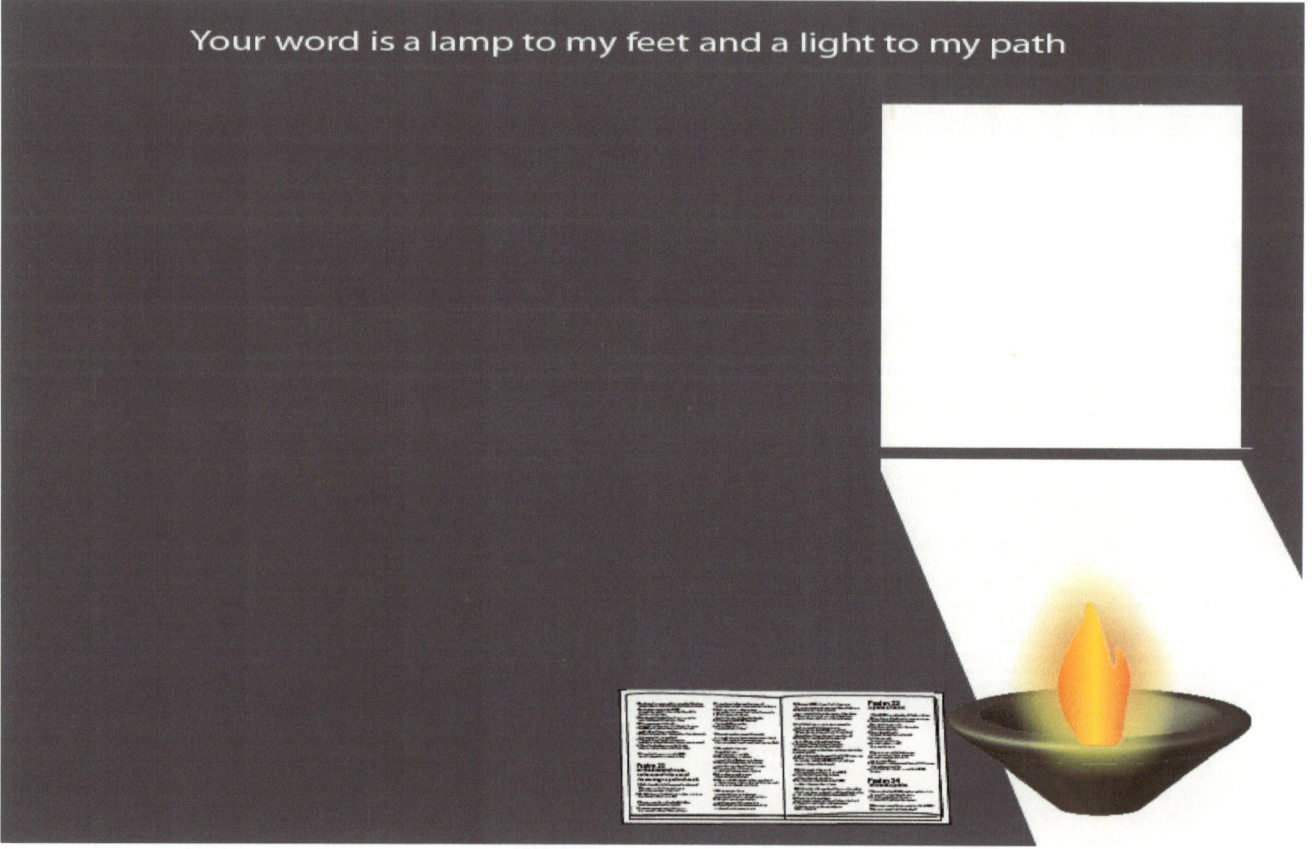

Practical Exercise

Let's try to hear God's audible voice.

Be ready to quiet your mind and listen.

Then write, draw, or record what God shows you.

Lesson 4: Feelings

Feelings

Your body will feel Him.

You will know He is speaking.

You may feel peace, joy, love.

You will feel when there is danger.

Feelings

Taste

Touch

Smell

It is strong and goes away when you listen.

Feelings

All of you who fear God, come and listen. I will tell you what he has done for me. I cried out to him with my mouth. I praised him with my tongue. If I had known of any sin in my heart, the Lord would not have listened to me. But God has listened. He has heard my prayer. Praise God. He did not ignore my prayer. He did not hold back his love from me. (Psalm 66:16-20)

Feelings

Make these people stubborn. Make them not able to understand what they hear and see. Otherwise, they might really understand what they see with their eyes and hear with their ears. They might really understand in their minds. If they did this, they would come back to me and be forgiven." (Isaiah 6:10 ICB)

Feelings

We need to be aware He is speaking.

Some people get shocks in their body like electricity.

You may feel some heat or cold.

God can use different parts of our body to make us know He is talking.

Types of Feelings

Some people feel God's presence.

You may feel Him when you pray.

You can feel Him close to you.

You may feel heavy or light.

Practical Exercise

Let's try to see if we can feel God and ask Him to touch us.

Wait for Him to touch us.

Lesson 5: Visions

Types of Visions

See Him, Jesus, Holy Spirit.

You will see places, people, things.

Things that will happen.

It is a clear image that is very real.

Lesson 5: Visions

Types of Visions

See Him, Jesus, Holy Spirit.

You will see places, people, things.

Things that will happen.

It is a clear image that is very real.

Visions

God will show you it again.

God will make it happen.

You cannot change it.

Pay attention to what He shows you.

Vision in the Bible

Then I looked up. And I saw a man holding a line for measuring things. I asked him, "Where are you going?"
He said to me, "I am going to measure Jerusalem. I will see how wide and how long it is." Then the angel who was talking with me left. And another angel came out to meet him. The second angel said to him, "Run and tell that young man this: 'Jerusalem will become a city without walls because there will be so many people and cattle in it. I will be a wall of fire around it,' says the Lord. 'And I will be the glory within it.' (Zechariah 2:1-5)

Vision in the Bible

Daniel's Vision

During the third year Belshazzar was king, I saw this vision. This was after the other one. In this vision I saw myself in the capital city of Susa. Susa is in the area of Elam. I was standing by the Ulai River. I looked up, and I saw a male sheep standing beside the river. It had two long horns. But one horn was longer than the other. The long horn was newer than the other horn. I watched the male sheep charge to the west. He also charged to the north and the south. No animal could stand before him. And none could save another animal from his power. He did whatever he wanted. And he became very powerful. While I was thinking about this, I saw a male goat come from the west. This goat had one large horn that was easy to see. It was between his eyes. He crossed over the whole earth. But his feet did not touch the ground. (Daniel 8:1-5)

More about Visions

We see them any time of the day or night.

We can be taken to another place and we unaware of time.

It is real as what we see and do.

God can show us things to come.

Types of Visions

Heaven

Place on Earth

Hell

Past, Present, and Future.

Practical Exercise

What vision did God give you?

We need to understand what it means.

Each thing we see is important.

Lesson 6: Dreams

Dreams

We see them any time of the day or night.

We can be taken to another place and we are unaware of time.

It is real as what we see and do.

God can show us things to come.

Dreams

Check if the dream is from you, God, or Satan.

God will show you it again if you need to know what to do.

God uses things and people in the dream to tell you something.

You cannot change it.

Dreams

When Gideon came to the enemy camp, he heard a man talking. That man was telling his friend about a dream. He was saying, "Listen, I dreamed that a loaf of barley bread rolled into the camp of Midian. It hit the tent so hard that the tent turned over and fell flat!" The man's friend said, "Your dream is about the sword of Gideon son of Joash, a man of Israel. God will let Gideon defeat Midian and the whole army!" (Judges 7: 13-14)

Dreams

But God warned the wise men in a dream not to go back to Herod. So they went home to their own country by a different way. (Matthew 2:12)

Jesus' Parents Take Him to Egypt
After they left, an angel of the Lord came to Joseph in a dream. The angel said, "Get up! Take the child and his mother and escape to Egypt. Herod will start looking for the child to kill him. Stay in Egypt until I tell you to return." (Matthew 2:13)

Types of Dreams

Normal: Feelings and thoughts (example: watching a movie)

Future: He shows you what will happen.
Danger
God gives you something.
God tells you what to do.
His presence.
Guides you.

Types of Dreams

Soul: Feelings, Attitudes, or What you Believe.

Unseen Fight: Make us free.
Pray better.
Show you the Devil's plans.
Bad dreams.
Warning of trouble.

Practical Exercise

What dream did God give you?

What did you dream about?

What we see is important.

Check with God's Word/Bible to find out.

Pray for what God showed you.

Lesson 7: God's Word/Bible

God's Word/Bible

We see them any time of the day or night.

We can be taken to another place and we unaware of time.

It is real as what we see and do.

God can show us things to come.

God's Word/Bible

You will know what He says you should do.

He will help you use His Word.

He will show you things from His Word.

He will tell you what to read.

God's Word/Bible

God says,
"I heard your prayers at the right time, and I gave you help on the day of salvation." (Isaiah 49:8)

Teach them to obey everything that I have told you. You can be sure that I will be with you always. I will continue with you until the end of the world." (Matthew 28:20 ICB)

God's Word/Bible

Rhema: It becomes alive and you can say it with your mouth.

Logos: God's word on paper and is seen with your eyes.

When God speaks in a still voice and audibly, it is rhema.

God uses both rhema and logos in dreams and visions.

When He uses thoughts, it is logos.

Practical Exercise

Let's ask God to speak to us through His Word.

What Bible verses did God give you?

Check with God's Word/Bible to find out.

Pray for yourself/the person for what God told you.

God's Word/Bible

Rhema: It becomes alive and you can say it with your mouth.

Logos: God's word on paper and is seen with your eyes.

When God speaks in a still voice and audibly, it is rhema.

God uses both rhema and logos in dreams and visions.

When He uses thoughts, it is logos.

Practical Exercise

Let's ask God to speak to us through His Word.

What Bible verses did God give you?

Check with God's Word/Bible to find out.

Pray for yourself/the person for what God told you.

Lesson 8: God's Thoughts

What are God's Thoughts?

They are always true, kingly, good, clean, right, loving, and great or worthy to be praised.

His thoughts are higher than our thinking.

God's thoughts are many.

Thoughts

He gives you ideas, art, songs, dance, picture, more.

Plans and directs you.

Teach you things.

He will remind you about things, places and people.

Thoughts

He will tell you where to go and what to do.

Words come to your mind.

He will remind you of things you forgot.

He will repeat it.

Thoughts

The Lord says, "Your thoughts are not like my thoughts. Your ways are not like my ways. (Isaiah 55:8)

As the Scripture says, "Who has known the mind of the Lord? Who has been able to give the Lord advice? (Romans 11:34 ICB)

Lord, you have done such great things! How deep are your thoughts! (Psalm 92:5)

Thoughts

The Spirit knows all things, even the deep secrets of God. It is like this: No one knows the thoughts that another person has. Only a person's spirit that lives in him knows his thoughts. It is the same with God. No one knows the thoughts of God. Only the Spirit of God knows God's thoughts. (1 Corinthians 2:4)

Thoughts

The Lord says, "Your thoughts are not like my thoughts. Your ways are not like my ways. (Isaiah 55:8)

As the Scripture says, "Who has known the mind of the Lord? Who has been able to give the Lord advice? (Romans 11:34 ICB)

Lord, you have done such great things! How deep are your thoughts! (Psalm 92:5)

Thoughts

The Spirit knows all things, even the deep secrets of God. It is like this: No one knows the thoughts that another person has. Only a person's spirit that lives in him knows his thoughts. It is the same with God. No one knows the thoughts of God. Only the Spirit of God knows God's thoughts. (1 Corinthians 2:4)

God's Promise

"After this, I will give my Spirit freely to all kinds of people. Your sons and daughters will prophesy. Your old men will dream dreams. Your young men will see visions. At that time I will give my Spirit even to servants, both men and women. (Joel 2:28)

Practical Exercise

Let's ask God what thoughts He has for us.

Check with God's Word/Bible to find out.

Pray for yourself/the person for what God told you.

Lesson 9: Gift of Prophecy

The Gift of Prophecy

What is it?

It is to give or receive a word from God about the future.

It tells us what God wants to do in our life.

We need to pray for it to happen and obey God.

Follow God's instructions.

The Gift of Prophecy

Expect that you will walk in the prophecy.

Focus on walking with God.

Trust that He will lead you to see it happen.

There is a time you may have to wait a long time before it happens.

The Gift of Prophecy

God may have to change you before you experience the prophecy happen.

You need to be at the right place at the right time.

Know the season you are in (growth, change, healing, etc.)

The Gift of Prophecy

"After this, I will give my Spirit freely to all kinds of people. Your sons and daughters will prophesy. Your old men will dream dreams. Your young men will see visions. At that time I will give my Spirit even to servants, both men and women. (Joel 2:28)

The Gift of Prophecy

and to another the effecting of miracles, and to another prophecy, and to another the distinguishing of spirits, to another various kinds of tongues, and to another the interpretation of tongues.(1 Corinthians 12:10)

For we know in part and we prophesy in part;
(1 Corinthians 13:9)

The Gift of Prophecy

"After this, I will give my Spirit freely to all kinds of people. Your sons and daughters will prophesy. Your old men will dream dreams. Your young men will see visions. At that time I will give my Spirit even to servants, both men and women. (Joel 2:28)

The Gift of Prophecy

and to another the effecting of miracles, and to another prophecy, and to another the distinguishing of spirits, to another various kinds of tongues, and to another the interpretation of tongues.(1 Corinthians 12:10)

For we know in part and we prophesy in part;
(1 Corinthians 13:9)

The Gift of Prophecy

God gives us the Holy Spirit to speak to us His secrets.

Holy Spirit is the one that has the gifts and gives them to us.

We use different gifts for each person who needs God's help.

We only know one part of what God is going to do in the future.

Practical Exercise

Find somebody to ask God to speak to you about them.

Does it sound like God?

Check with God's Word/Bible to find out.

Pray for yourself/the person for what God told you.

Lesson 10: Others

Others

God gives us words, pictures, songs, and more when we help others.

He also gives ideas when we worship Him in church.

He also speaks to us during the time we pray for others.

We need to tell others what He tells us at the right time.

Others

You can have Bible study with others.

God will speak to us how He wants us to help others.

He will tell us what to pray with others.

Others

You should have other people with you to do God's work.

Always ask God before you work with others.

He gives them gifts that will work with you.

Others may have a word, picture, and more for you.

Others

Acts 18:27

When he (Apollos) wanted to travel to Achaia, the brothers and sisters encouraged him and wrote to the disciples so they would open their homes to him. Once he arrived, he was of great help to those who had come to believe through grace.

Others

Mark 3:18

Peter, John, James, and Andrew; Philip and Thomas; Bartholomew and Matthew; James, Alphaeus' son; Simon the zealot; and Judas, James' son— all were united in their devotion to prayer, along with some women, including Mary the mother of Jesus, and his brothers.

Ask about Others

Ask Jesus who are the people He wants you to work with.

Ask Him to lead you to those who need to speak into your life.

Ask Him who He wants you to help.

Practical Exercise

Find somebody to ask God to speak to you about them.

Does it sound like God?

Check with God's Word/Bible to find out.

Pray for the person for what God told you.

Lesson 11: Jesus

Jesus

Jesus loves to talk to you one on one.

He may come to you in a dream, vision, speak to you in a still small voice, audibly, feelings, thoughts, and God's Word.

We need to come to Jesus every day to ask Him to speak to us.

Do what He tells you.

Jesus

Ask Jesus who are the people He wants you to work with.

Ask Him to lead you to those who need to speak into your life.

Ask Him who He wants you to help.

Jesus

Jesus always speaks in love.

He is your brother, best friend, king, and in the Bible He is the Bridegroom.

He wants us to be open with Him.

Jesus has much to say to us.

Practical Exercise

Ask Jesus to speak to you.

Does it sound like Him?

Check with God's Word/Bible to find out.

Pray for yourself and anyone else for what God told you.

Lesson 12: Holy Spirit and His gifts

Holy Spirit and His gifts

He is gentle and loving.

He will tell you about Jesus.

He will remind you who Jesus is.

Holy Spirit and His gifts

The gifts of the Holy Spirit:

Wisdom, understanding, counsel, boldness, knowledge, piety (loyalty), and fear of the Lord.

Word of wisdom, Word of knowledge, gift of prophecy, distinguishing of spirits, faith, healing, miracles, unknown words (tongues), translation of tongues.

Dreams and visions.

Holy Spirit and His gifts

He is the singing spirit.

He is the Counselor, Teacher, Comforter, Guide, and much more.

You can get to know Him more and be close with Him.

He will also tell you and remind you of what God wants you to know.

Practical Exercise

Find somebody to ask the Holy Spirit to speak to you.

Does it sound like the Holy Spirit?

Check with God's Word/Bible to find out.

Pray for yourself and anyone else for what God told you.

Prayer

Father God, Jesus, and Holy Spirit, thank you for talking to me. Please let me always hear you every day and to do what pleases you. Guide me and protect me. Bring me to the right places and people. Help me to bring people to know you and to speak to them your words. That they will accept it in Jesus' name. Amen.

Salvation Prayer

Dear God, I know that I am a sinner. I believe that Jesus Christ died on the cross to pay for my sins and that He rose from the grave after 3 days. That through Him I can have long-lasting life. I surrender myself to you and ask Jesus Christ to come into my heart to be my Personal Lord and Savior. I receive your eternal life and choose to live for you. I am willing to yield myself to you and let you work in me. Cleanse me with the blood of Jesus Christ. Teach and lead my steps. Deliver me from all sins, transgressions, iniquities, curses, and bondage. Fill me up. Baptize me with the Holy Spirit and with fire in Jesus' name. Amen.

Holy Spirit Baptism Prayer

Holy Spirit, I welcome you to come into my life. Jesus I believe that you are the Baptizer. Please baptize me with your Holy Spirit and with fire for your glory in Jesus name. Arrest my tongue to speak for you in Jesus name to release out the words you want to impart to me in Jesus name.' Amen.

Message from the Author

Thank you for taking the time to learn How to Hear God's Voice. You are now ready to listen to the Lord. You can use this guide to teach others how to hear God for themselves. It is highly recommended that they get a copy of the books, so that they will know the steps and ways God speaks, so they can prepare their hearts to learn and practice the principles. The Lord speak to you clearly. It is advised to practice this daily. It is to grow your ability to hear Him, so that you will be sharp. For the days are coming that we must know when He is calling to us to come with Him.

Biography

Chelsea Kong is a writer, creative arts and digital media artist, and skilled administrative professional. She was born and raised in Windsor, Ontario. She moved to Toronto in 2003. She also has served in her local church in a variety of roles from audiovisual, photography, to assisting on the worship team, and ministry team. She also has a passion for families being united. Her writing consists of children's books, stories, bridal writing, poems, lyrics for songs, words of encouragement, blessings, prayers, and jokes. She is the author of the Bridal Collection, Knowing God, How to Hear God's Voice, New Life in Jesus, Loving Israel, God's Gifts, Meeting God, Word Power, Fruit of the Spirit, The Tabernacle, Bride for Jesus, A Life of Prayer, etc. She also has her own Bible Puzzle books and other inspired products. She also has a podcast channel called Chelsea K on Anchorfm and her podcasts are found on YouTube. Chelsea has been on Unity Live Radio, The Lady Tracey Show, and will be on Susie's CoffeeTime.

Other Products

The Bridal Collection
Knowing God
How to Hear God's Voice
New Life in Jesus
Loving Israel
God's Gifts
Meeting God
Word Power
Fruit of the Spirit
The Tabernacle
Bride for Jesus
A Life of Prayer
Live Free
Who am I in Jesus
Walk in Love
God's Favor
Man of God
Woman of God
How to Use Money
God's Wisdom
Fasting
See Jerusalem and Bethany
First Fruit Offering
Pentecost
Feast of Trumpets
Day of Atonement
Feast of Tabernacles
Counting the Omer
Festival of Lights
Glory, Presence, and Holy Spirit
Live in God's Presence

31 Day Devotional
Biblical Puzzle Book Vol 1
Biblical Puzzle Book Vol 2
Biblical Puzzle Book Vol 3
Biblical Puzzle Book Vol 4
Biblical Puzzle Book Vol 5
Bible Puzzles for Young Children Book 1
Biblie Puzzles for Young Children Book 2
Bible Puzzles for Young Children Book 3
Biblical Puzzles for Children Book 1
Biblical Puzzles for Children Book 2
Biblical Puzzles for Children Book 3

Teaching Series
How to Hear God's Voice Teaching Guide
Relationship with God, Jesus,
Holy Spirit Guide

Teaching (Non-Sale)
Purim
Passover
Resurrection

And much more!

Please check Chelsea's website for links to other books and products found on Amazon, Barnes and Noble, and Kobo. Please leave a review to help the author to write more books. Thank you!

https://chelseak532002550.wordpress.com
https://www.youtube.com/channel/UCOvw9wUmkE08Akeq2z3TQVA

Coaching Products

Teaching Series Packages to train you to equip you for God's purpose!

Check the website for details:
https://chelseak532002550.wordpress.com

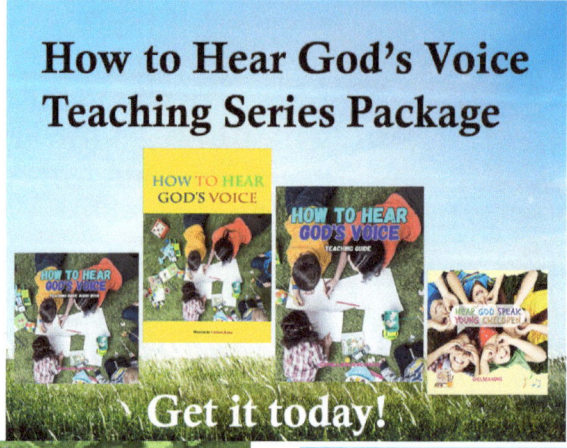

Learn How to Hear God's Voice
Knowing Him
Build a Relationship with Him

Each package includes lessons and related books

www.ingramcontent.com/pod-product-compliance
Lightning Source LLC
Chambersburg PA
CBHW041417010526
44107CB00016B/1202